Another Book of Parkinality Poetry

Another Book of Parkinality Poetry

The Parkinality Poet

Copyright © 2020 Julie Walker

The moral right of the author has been asserted.

This book is not intended as a substitute for the medical advice of physicians. The reader should regularly consult a physician in matters relating to his/her health and particularly with respect to any symptoms that may require diagnosis or medical attention.

Apart from any fair dealing for the purposes of research or private study, or criticism or review, as permitted under the Copyright, Designs and Patents Act 1988, this publication may only be reproduced, stored or transmitted, in any form or by any means, with the prior permission in writing of the publishers, or in the case of reprographic reproduction in accordance with the terms of licences issued by the Copyright Licensing Agency. Enquiries concerning reproduction outside those terms should be sent to the publishers.

Matador
9 Priory Business Park,
Wistow Road, Kibworth Beauchamp,
Leicestershire. LE8 0RX
Tel: 0116 279 2299
Email: books@troubador.co.uk
Web: www.troubador.co.uk/matador
Twitter: @matadorbooks

ISBN 978 1838594 763

British Library Cataloguing in Publication Data.
A catalogue record for this book is available from the British Library.

Typeset in 10pt Georgia by Troubador Publishing Ltd, Leicester, UK

Matador is an imprint of Troubador Publishing Ltd

For... my mum and Louise.

Contents

Welcome	viii

Damon, Sheila and Ben

Babs: Damon	2
Surprize: Sheila	3
Equality: Anon	4
The elixir of life: Damon and Sheila	6
Family and PD: Damon	8
Still the same: Ben age 7 ¾	10
Brain buzz: Damon	12
Family tradition: Damon, Ben and son	14

Joanna, Ross and Molly

Ready for the day: Joanna	18
All change: Joanna and Ross	19
More to life: Ross	20
Mouse in the house: Joanna	22
Just two steps: Joanna	24
Sometimes: Molly age 7	26
Together: Joanna and Ross	27
Not a sprint: Molly age 18	28

Deirdre, Terrance and Sam

Swimming pool rules: Terrance	32
Silence please: Deirdre	34
Dog son: Terrance and Sam	35
Feel the fear: Deirdre	36
Vital for life: Deirdre	37

Chaos: Deirdre   38
Unwanted lodger: Deirdre and Terrance   39
Inevitability: Deirdre   40

Lucy
Idiots: Lucy   42
Lucy Lemon's daughter: Anon   44
Mystery guest: Lucy   45
Save our planet: Lucy   46
Compulsion: Lucy   48
Look inside: Lucy   49

Margery and Melvin
Fuss pot: Margery   52
The good 'ole days: Melvyn   53
Sod the difference: Margery and Melvyn   54
Keep your distance: Margery   55
Repeat prescription: Melvyn   56
Alert: Margery   57
Absorption: Margery   58
Feeling better?: Margery and Melvyn   59
Facade: Margery and Melvyn   60

Imagine: Support group   61

I am not medically trained   62
What is Parkinson's Disease?   64
What is Parkinality?   67
Thank you   68

Profound: The Parkinality Poet   69

Welcome to Another Book of Parkinality Poetry: Why? Oh, PD

Before you read this book
there are some things I'd like to say
please read and absorb
then go on your merry way

The characters in the poems
have all been created by me
you won't meet them in the high street
you can't invite them round for tea

YOPD is woven through the pages
but, please don't run a mile
the poems are interesting and entertaining
and some might make you smile

If you live with Parkinson's Disease
some verses might strike a chord with you
written for greater awareness
the ultimate aim is a cure

Please note
I don't wear a lab coat
I didn't go to med school
so, if you need information and advice
consult a medical professional

Parkinson's Disease (PD) is a (currently) incurable degenerative neurological disease.

Young Onset Parkinson's Disease (YOPD) refers to those diagnosed with Parkinson's Disease (PD) before they are fifty.

The Parkinality Poet, aka Janet Bric-a-Brac, aka Julie Walker

www.parkinality.co.uk

Damon, Sheila and Ben

Babs
Damon

"Babs is a dark horse"
Damon let slip the other day
he'd been following the form
today was her big day

Leaving the parade ring
Damon breaks into a smile
Babs looks restless, but ready
for the Rowley Mile

Encouraged into the stalls
thundering down the track
blinkered against distraction
never looking back

His instincts had been right
Damon breaks into a smile
Babs is leading by a nose
on the Rowley Mile

Approaching the final furlong
was his confidence misplaced?
He watches as she loses ground
he'd backed a win, not a place

Neck and neck at the finishing post
Damon breaks into a smile
a win, confirmed by a photo finish
on the Rowley Mile

Surprize
Sheila

Mesmerising us
moving to-and-fro
persuading us
to have a go

To-and-fro
tuppence sent down the slide

To-and-fro
tuppence lands on its side

To-and-fro
tuppence teeters on the ledge

To-and-fro
tuppence falls over the edge

Is there hope?
Is there a glimmer?
Nervously peeking
yes, she's a winner

So, what's Sheila's
first win for a while?
It's a plastic pile of poo
wearing a smile

Equality
Anon

Today, men and women
live quite equal lives
women can be plumbers
men can be housewives

But there's still one thing
which causes debate
something men love
something women hate

Boys often want one
at secondary school
thinking girls will love it
thinking they'll look cool

Women often get one
at around thirty-two
wondering why
wondering what they should do

It takes no effort
not even a little bit
ideal for a lazy man
ideal for a hippy chick

Men spend time
making it look great
women remove it
before going on a date

On Damon it could look good
on Sheila a little weird
not everyone looks great
with a moustache and a beard

The elixir of life
Damon and Sheila

Damon got a call at three thirty-three
from a lady shouting, "Please help me"
Sheila's phone rang at four forty-four
the lady now sobbing, "Water's flowing across the floor"

Sheila arrived first – more speed less haste
Damon arrived late – more haste less speed

Sheila peered out from under the sink
Damon gave her a cheeky wink
her dungarees had caught his eye
"Pass me a spanner," she said with a sigh

At work Sheila was one of the men
in the pub she was also one of them
a plumber, their work mate
no one had ever asked her on a date

Shower, pipe, tap, drain
Damon asked, "Can I see you again?"
Drip, block, burst, flow
Sheila replied categorically, "No"

She'd bitten her nails down to the quick
she'd started to wear a little lipstick
she always kept her hair squeaky clean
she hoped she didn't look too keen

Trickle, plink, gush, rain
Damon asked, "Can I see you again?"
Clean, wash, drink, thirst
Sheila relented – "Yes" – she could do worse

After three burst pipes and a false alarm
Damon proposed by a reservoir near his uncle's farm
their love had blossomed over a torrent of water
they were now happily married with one son

Family and PD
Damon

"We were two, now we're three
the uninvited guest; Parkinson's Disease"

Parkinson's was furthest from my mind
I wasn't old with a tremor, that's not being unkind
a family man, with a son and a wife
just forty-two and in the prime of my life

When switched on and working well
I almost forget about being unwell
almost, because PD is constantly there
bubbling away, it just doesn't care

I dream of a time, when a cure is found
when I will no longer stick out from the crowd
people will look and not see PD
people will look and actually see me

I'll sleep soundly from ten 'til seven
those nine hours' rest will be absolute heaven
I'll smile and give a cheeky wink
stop worrying what people think

If I stagger whilst out on the town
it'll be beer, not PD, which makes me fall down
I'll still avoid spaghetti, it's messy you see
both with and without Parkinson's Disease

Until then, I'm unreliable and unsteady
impatience goes with the territory
unpredictable, life is difficult today
I wish Parkinson's would just go away

Sheila is the love of my life, the one
Ben is our beautiful only son
they also have to live with PD
they're also victims, not just me

Still the same
Ben age 7¾

Luke and I are both nearly eight
Mum says, "Double trouble,"; he's my mate
once we smuggled a toad into class
I've never seen Miss Smith move so fast

Each day we walk home from school
stopping at the park to play football
last Friday, Luke made me sad
he said, "Why is your mum turning into your dad?"

My mum helps out each week at Scouts
she drives Luke and I about
my mum irons my shirts, she cooks my tea
last week my mum tried to climb a tree

Luke's dad helps out each week at Scouts
he drives Luke and me about
Luke's mum irons his shirts, she cooks his tea
I bet Luke's mum has never climbed a tree

I told Luke, my dad's still the same
we still support the same football team
we still share a pie at half-time
we still cheer from the touchline

I told Luke, when Parkinson's stops my dad
he has some tricks to get his walking back
my dad gives me a signal, sometimes a wink
I'll grab his hand and we'll start to sprint

I told Luke, when dad freezes, people stop to assist
my dad said one rude man thought he was drunk
sometimes I get scared, but my dad makes it fun
I love it, when we break into a run

Brain buzz
Damon

The nights are long, Damon feels so low
he should've been asleep long ago

His mind is awake, his body is asleep
just reached 453 sheep
still no rest, no let-up in this buzz
his brain is awake, yet full of fuzz

Damon wants to sleep, he needs to
his brain doesn't know what to do
his body is stiff, his arm is in pain
simply needing to feel human again

Why in this world of speed and light
is the night so dark? It doesn't seem right
the day works so unbelievably well
so why does the night feel like hell?

Constantly moving, rocked to the core
Damon doesn't think he can take much more
finally, a glint, a spark of light
to mark the end of this never-ending night

Family tradition
Damon, Ben and son

Leaving home at one
wrapped in a scarf
in the late summer sun

Joining the chant
the crush at the gate
the cup in our sight
it's never too late

My dad sups a pint
we share a pie
that ritual was ours
my dad and I

Shoulder to shoulder
until eighty-three
when we won the title
two goals to three

Leaving home at one
wrapped in a scarf
in the late summer sun

Joining the chant
the crush at the gate
the cup in our sight
it's never too late

I sup a pint
we share a pie
now that ritual is ours
my son and I

Joanna, Ross and Molly

Ready for the day
Joanna

Joanna was feeling rather good
ready for the day
the sun was shining in the sky
it was time to make some hay

Arriving at the ticket gate
stopped in her tracks
trying not to panic
trying desperately to relax

Commuters barge past her
focussed on the daily race
avoiding the eyes of the lady
with tears streaming down her face

Shuffling and staggering
onto the waiting train
collapsing into a seat
exhausted again

Feeling relatively normal
enjoying the calm
wondering what was wrong
why her body had raised the alarm

All change
Joanna and Ross

Commuting together, yet sitting apart
Ross noticed Joanna right from the start
high-street suits weren't his usual style
he fell in love with her beautiful smile

Briefly conversing when he trod on her toe
squealing, "Ouch," muttering, "I've got to go"
those words weren't plucked from a passionate play
but the memory of that moment lingers today

Ross made her smile, there was a spark
a summer of long lunches and walks in the park
that was when the romance began
when he became her man

Ross was a leader, a man amongst men
Joanna became his wife, a true mother hen
that was their public persona, the politician and his wife
at home they were a team with the perfect life

Recently symptoms had been circling her mind
Joanna wasn't usually the worrying kind
results were back from the men in white coats
they waited as the doctor read through her notes

Leaning on the desk, the doctor looked into her eyes
with just three words, he changed their lives:
"You have Parkinson's," but he didn't know why
Ross held her hand, Joanna began to cry

More to life
Ross

Ross checks in the mirror
Joanna straightens his tie
Molly hugs her daddy
they wave him goodbye

A surge of sound hits him
like a tidal wave
the wall of noise will haunt him
today until his grave

Walking to the waiting car
not a word passes his lips
despite the questions
profanities and the quips

Placards taunt him
proclaiming the people's views
desperation in their eyes
this could be front-page news

More hospitals, more schools
definitely less crime
then the realisation struck him:
"Their demands are the same as mine"

Time stood still
for a moment or two
turning his back
he knew what he had to do

He wanted to explain
that he wanted the same thing
that his priorities
were gradually changing

Ross returned to the house
into the arms of his wife
he would resign immediately
there must be more to life

Mouse in the house
Joanna

I am getting tiny
really rather small
like a little mouse
hardly there at all

My voice is getting quieter
really rather weak
all I can manage
is a tiny little squeak

Strides are getting shorter
my feet drag the floor
taking all my strength
I try to reach the door

I place my hands on the wall
try to feel the way
my body moves, my feet don't
please don't fall, I pray

I lean and lunge
try to move away
try to make some progress
impossible today

I slip, I slide
I stumble
I just want to move
"It's so hard," I mumble

Once I walked through London
confident and proud
now I just want a cup of tea
is that allowed?

Tea at 3am?
That would be very nice
my legs won't move
I'm overtaken by some mice

I stop and think
do I really need that tea?
Is it really worth it?
I sink to my knees

This is Parkinson's
this is what it's like
lots of little challenges
another night of fight

When will a cure be found?
Goodness only knows
the mouse scuttles away
on its tiny little toes

Just two steps
Joanna

Another day is waking up
demanding control
how will I deal with it?
I'll have to let you know

Life is not a race
but there's a daily prize
which is waking at dawn
to watch the sunrise

Packed lunches made
I turn to cross the floor
just two more steps
just to reach the door

My feet freeze
my fingers won't bend
an invisible force
is taking control again

Just wave my girls off to school
'*just*' four letters, nothing deep
just cross the kitchen floor
I silently begin to weep

Am I asking for a lot?
Am I asking too much again?
My walking will return
I just don't know when

Count to ten, headphones on
the tunes are my technique
to try to distract the enemy
and move my fingers and feet

Slowly beginning to move
rhythms start to fill my head
motion gradually returns
my legs stop feeling like lead

Struggling to the front door
to wave the girls on their way
each moment is different
tomorrow is another day

Sometimes
Molly age 7

Sometimes she's slow
sometimes she's a busy bee
sometimes her fingers fumble
when she tries to help me

Sometimes she's quiet
sometimes she tries to shout
sometimes her words are wobbly
they just won't come out

Sometimes she's a fidget
sometimes she wiggles like a fish
sometimes she can't sit still
just like my little sis

Sometimes her face is cross
sometimes her smile hides
sometimes her eyes are sad
she said she's happy inside

I really truly love my mummy
she is everything to me
but I really don't like her having
Parkinson's Disease

Together
Joanna and Ross

"Parkinson's is slowly changing me
it's become an obsession, a reason to be"

Today, Joanna's always busy
but things are never done
she won't let Parkinson's drag her down
she *will* still have some fun

Ross and Joanna are a team
dedicated as husband and wife
moving forward together
their family are their life

"Parkinson's is here to stay
I'd give anything for one disease-free day"

Not a sprint
Molly age 18

Frost beneath her feet
cheeks tender with the cold
should she really be here?
Was she being far too bold?

Pulling the bin bag round her
trying to catch her breath
should she really be here?
She could catch her death

She was now a number
she was no longer free
"I'm doing this for my mum
it's not all about me"

The first hour was bad
worse than she thought
she had to keep going
practise what she'd been taught

Beads on her brow
sweat on her chest
she had to keep going
keep doing her best

Surrounded by a menagerie
as far as her eyes could see
repeating to herself,
"It's not all about me"

The end was in sight
she was slow, but not last
she had never seen a phone box
moving so fast

The torture finally at an end
she was, almost, still alive
feeling like a superhero
Molly wore the cape with pride

Deirdre, Terrance and Sam

Swimming pool rules
Terrance

Terrance has been at the leisure centre
all of his working life
this place has shaped his world
it's where he met his wife

Deirdre was doing front crawl
his choice was butterfly
her swimming was rather slow
he wasn't going to lie

She wore an orange swimsuit
a hat with flowers round the rim
tight against her head
to stop the water getting in

If odd was the look, she was going for
she had certainly achieved that
he caught her eye, he was intrigued
then he threw it back

Swimming lessons, life-saving
timetables fill his head
his priority is water safety
ensuring that nobody *'leaves dead'*

Terrance parades around the pool
he's there to uphold the law
to keep the general public in line
school kids call him 'Terry the bore'

"Forgotten your kit?"
Today, teachers don't care
in his day kids would have to swim
in their stripy underwear

No running and no shouting
no diving, no petting too
this often confuses the kids
as they're nowhere near the zoo

Terrance has written a safety sign
which is more up to date
it doesn't beat about the bush
entitled, "Read before it's too late"

"Rules are made for a reason"
that's what the smart boy said
rules are there for a reason
that boy was bored out of his head

"Rules are made to be broken"
that's what the naughty boy said
rules are there to be broken
those were the last words that boy said

Silence please
Deirdre

Deirdre must walk for hours
she's not allowed to speak
striding silently and slowly
and her shoes mustn't squeak

Once a boy began to cry
Deirdre really did care
although she could only give him
a reassuring stare

She must curtail a cough
and swiftly silence a sneeze
which Deirdre often finds difficult
once she nearly wee'd

Deirdre must never laugh
a smile is where it starts
even if somebody burps
or accidentally... *breaks wind*

She has been employed
to keep an eye on the time
to give out instructions
to keep the students in line

At four Deirdre collects the papers
and sends them on their way
knowing they'll be reunited
on results day

Dog son
Terrance and Sam

Sit and then *lie down*
he drew the line at *beg*
Sam also refused to *roll over*
preferring to *wave* instead

Walking to heel was easy
not a collar in sight
Terrance didn't have a problem using a lead
but he thought social services might

They stopped for lunch at twelve
Deirdre made sandwiches with jam
she didn't want to risk the wrong cheese
Terrance was a such a pedantic man

Terrance attended every practice
Fido slept through all four
Terrance was quietly confident
as he carefully closed the front door

Walking into the arena
Fido was the star of the show
Sam was left at home with the 'ump
he should've been allowed to go

Terrance brought home two rosettes
Deirdre was delighted they'd won
but wished he'd practised with Fido, the dog
rather than Sam, their youngest son

Feel the fear
Deirdre

Hidden for months
never mentioning a word
would he understand?
Don't be absurd

Deirdre was worried
how would Terrance react?
How would he deal with her diagnosis?
How would he deal with the facts?

She was concerned about the future
she worried more and more
convinced when Terrance found out
he would walk straight out the door

Her balance was getting worse
symptoms becoming difficult to hide
the day was fast approaching
when Terrance would discover her lie

Slipping tablets into her pocket
hiding Parkinson's drugs in her drawer
she must take the medication
for now, Terrance need know nothing more

Vital for life
Deirdre

Vital for life but not well known
it cannot be farmed or intensively grown

It's something you can't see, taste or smell
but without it you'd be extremely unwell

Got it?
You won't know or care
just be grateful it's still there

Lack it?
Rigid and still
don't panic, just take another pill

We need to find a way and find it quick
of making dopamine in the kitchen sink

Who?
What?
Why?
Where?

You know, we really don't care

Chaos
Deirdre

As the switch is flicked
let the chaos begin
carefully shut the door
please don't come in

Hidden from prying eyes
never sharing the pain
please make this stop
so, I can be me again

My body slows
as the power goes down
waiting to reconnect
the hub and the town

If you haven't got it
you won't get it

If you haven't got it
how could you possibly know?

How could you possibly see
what it feels like to be me?

The moment will pass
I don't know when
the moment will pass
when I can be me again

Unwanted lodger
Deirdre and Terrance

An unwanted lodger
on a long-term let
an unwanted lodger
they wish they'd never met

Parkinson's is taking the love
taking the sun
gradually taking
all they have become

Inevitability
Deirdre

Deirdre cooked a meal
he stayed out late

Terrance danced 'til dawn
she cleared just one plate

He had one last drink
she drank alone

Deirdre tried to ring
Terrance had switched off his phone

Lucy

Idiots
Lucy

Blinking in the half-light
hardly a wink of sleep
glancing to her left:
"Goodness, who was that creep?"

Lucy slowly recalling
yesterday's events
one thing was for sure
he wasn't heaven sent

They met at midday
at least she remembered that
or was it midnight?
She started to doubt her facts

Lonely, but not alone
both needing to have some fun
she had a shot of vodka
he had a double rum

Those hours were a blur of
cards and dice and drink
inhibitions left at the door
they didn't even think

What had she done?
This wasn't on her bucket list
Lucy only excuse was that
she'd been extremely *drunk*

Lucy was full of regret
why had she ignored her brain?
She wasn't usually that type of girl
she hoped she never saw him again

Lucy Lemon's daughter

Lucy Lemon's daughter was ready to have some fun
she pulled on her wellies
skipped into the autumn sun

Lucy Lemon's daughter, had just turned six
she loved going to the stream
to play floating sticks

Lucy was miles away
remembering when life began
never met, never seen
born with another man

Lucy could offer nothing
she felt she had no choice
the decisions were made
long before her daughter had a voice

Lucy Lemon's daughter, wore just one stripy glove
until a lady stopped and asked,
"Is this yours, love?"

Lucy Lemon's daughter giggled on the blue horse
rocked backwards and forwards
by her adopted mum, of course

Mystery guest
Lucy

Unpredictable, unfathomable
Lucy didn't understand
what was ruling her life
with an invisible hand

Arguing or bantering
Lucy didn't care which
this silent treatment was
driving her round the twist

Her symptoms were unpredictable
they confused her GP
after some simple tests
the neurologist diagnosed PD

Lucy was suffering from
information overload
she needed to tell
she needed to offload

After a couple of hours
on the telephone
she wasn't lonely
but she was definitely alone

Save our planet
Lucy

New is so last year
second-hand is so today
old is so tomorrow
that's what the fashionistas say

Charity shops are frequented
by those in the know
a couple of quid for
an on-trend fashion show

Lucy bought a dress
originally half a crown
relabelled *vintage*
it becomes a *retro* gown

This planet needs saving
"Who's responsible for this mess?"
Lucy hangs her head in shame
she got a carrier for her retro dress

Lucy will repair and reuse
but could do more
the paint she bought was eco
cost ten pounds more

She also spent a fortune
on a new recycling bin
but the packaging that it came in
really was a sin

Today people will pay more
for something painted green
also labelled artisan
the price becomes obscene

Money makes the word go around
not gravitational force
do we upgrade and recycle?
...of course

Jumping on the bandwagon
it's a new marketplace
meaning huge corporations
keep a smile on their face

Compulsion
Lucy

Lucy has a compulsion
to buy stuff every day
spiralling out of control
nothing will get in her way

Shelves full of stilettos
flats flooding the floor
cupboard crammed with shoes
she can't shut the door

Funds running low
she picks up the phone
to ring the man on the telly
advertising the loan

She has shoes on her feet
but the larder is bare
Lucy has no time to eat
but she doesn't really care

What has happened to her?
Lucy wasn't like this before
she always had self-control
before Parkinson's broke down the door

Look inside
Lucy

Lucy, sixty-four, left on the shelf
no family, no friends and in ill health
neighbours thought they'd done their bit
staring at her front door, never knocking on it

If the rumour mill had got its facts straight
if her neighbours had bothered to knock and wait
they'd have been quick to discover
they should never judge a book by its cover

Lucy had won and lost
been an absent mother, a demanding boss
always a lover, never a wife
today she still retains her zest for life

She spends her days giving advice
sharing fashion tips from her long life
teenage problems hadn't changed that much
just language: *bae* was once a *crush*

Lucy has gone viral, has her own hashtag
contributing to an online, on-trend mag
she's certainly not dull, just ill and old
sixty is the new twenty, or so we're told

Lucy tweets about what is *on fleek*
to her followers she's *Lucy the internet geek*

Margery and Melvyn

Fuss pot
Margery

"Hi, I'm Margery, twenty-eight this year
I love punk music, prefer red wine to beer
I'm six feet tall, so no short guys
and you must have piercing blue eyes
I enjoy theatre, particularly musicals
and I work part time at two local schools"

"Hello, I'm Margery, aged thirty-two
I'm looking for someone just like you
I want to go out, have a good time
watch punk bands, drink good red wine
I enjoy all types of theatre; I don't mind what
and I also have a part-time job"

"Morning, I'm Marg, forty-five years young
I'm searching for that special someone
I like everyone and I love everything
if we had a race, I'd let you win
I'd love to share a bottle of good red wine
please take me out, I'm free any time"

"Hi, I'm Margery, sixty-two
if you've got a pulse, then you'll do"

The good 'ole days
Melvyn

Melvyn Crisp was a thief with a lisp
in the days when stealing was fun
thinking back to those halcyon days
when he could simply 'grab and run'

Then he would shout, "Stop thief"
to distract the security man
leaving Melvyn to empty the shop
then drive off in the getaway van

Technology has now taken over
man has been replaced by TV
Melvyn was disappointed to discover
that it was closed circuit, not reality

The internet offers new opportunities
in modern-day crime
but Melvyn heard he could catch a virus
if caught shoplifting online

So, he decided to get a proper job
becoming a warden in the zoo
this leopard could never change his spots
need a giraffe? Melvyn can get you two

Sod the difference
Margery and Melvyn

Tall
blonde
not that young
Margery loves good red wine and having fun

Short
slim
extremely hirsute
Melvyn loves whitebait and playing the flute

She loathes spiders
she prefers roast beef
she enjoys musicals
she grinds her teeth

He hates punk music
he prefers a bath
he loves Margate
he snorts when he laughs

Their first date was over chocolate cake
Margery knew something was amiss
when Melvyn said he had Parkinson's
she thought he was *being sarcastic*

Incompatible on paper
the perfect match in real life
shredding the A4
they became husband and wife

Keep your distance
Margery

From a distance if you squint
Margery looks quite good today
get too close and you'll see
her roots are completely grey

With Parkinson's she often
has to make a choice
"Should I brush my teeth or wash my hair?"
she asks in a whispered voice

She would plait her underarm hair
but that would be difficult to do
bad dexterity makes tasks impossible
her sister simply didn't have a clue

Margery is far from squeaky clean
preferring to dance the night away
leaving her personal hygiene
to another rainy day

Repeat prescription
Melvyn

Melvyn finds life amusing
simple things make him laugh
such as poultry crossing the road
or jokes about giraffes

Sniggers sweep through his body
like wildfire through the trees
if Melvyn laughs a little too hard
don't be surprised if he wees

Bodily functions, talking dogs
slapstick and smelly cheese
all make him laugh so much
they can bring him to his knees

He was once told a joke so funny
he was rolling on the floor
his laugh became hysterical
realising he'd heard that one before

Laughter might increase dopamine
inside his broken brain
which could help him move
feel slightly more human again

Laughter is the best medicine
although it doesn't cure any ills
it might help Melvyn feel better
along with his many Parkinson's pills

Alert
Margery

Margery listens for the alarm
anticipates the sound
loud enough to wake the dead?
Please don't clown around

Take them in an instant
don't wait a second more
don't finish what you're doing
Parkinson's meds are such a bore

Without those tiny tablets
life wouldn't be the same
those pills help keep us moving
stop Parkinson's driving us insane

Absorption
Margery

Don't swallow all your pills at once
don't take them too quick
and when you take them
don't skimp on the drink

Too little water, they'll miss the spot
sinking before they can swim
too much water, you might wee a lot
but at least they'll be absorbed right in

Into the gut up to the brain
which is tricky, please don't frown
speed is of the essence
but please don't turn us upside down

Feeling better?
Margery and Melvyn

Negativity is a disaster
the cold makes us feel worse
stress might make us freeze
all three are the Parkinson's curse

What do you suggest we do?
Sit at home and mope?
Do we do that?
One word: "Nope"

We would dance with the milkman
a neighbour or their friend
we're really not that fussy
although a refusal will offend

We will hit the highest note
then warble one down low
our repertoire is limited
these are the only notes we know

Music is amazing
but it can't cure any ills
it can help in combination
with our Parkinson's pills

Facade
Margery and Melvyn

Coat on, shoes on
in their dreams
this is not how it happens
all is not what it seems

Head up, chin up
put on a smile
pretend to be well
for a short while

Fall through the door
have a quick drink
unsteady on their feet
it's not what you think

Dance 'til they can't
taking over the space
dance 'til they can't
with smiles on their face

Falling out the door
struggling along the street
saying hello to
everyone they meet

Finally reaching home
falling through the door
Parkinson's tries to take control
they can't take much more

Imagine
Support group

A warm welcome
a friendly face
feeling safe
in this special place

Singing together
laughing out loud
with new friends
you're part of the crowd

Easing the pain
breathing the air
sensing the calm
where people care

Talking it through
going the extra mile
a challenging day
ends with a reassuring smile

You have reached the end of the stories ... now for my 'the same size as the rest of the book' print.

I am not medically trained.
I am an ordinary person dealing with an awful disease.

Please speak to a medical professional for information, advice and to talk through anything which is worrying you. Please, do not make changes or start anything new unless you are under the guidance of your medical professional.

Everyone diagnosed with Parkinson's Disease is different; disease progression and symptoms will vary from person to person.

All of the poems, people, families, situations and relationships in this book are fictional.

Any information I give is merely my personal opinion. Some of my work may turn out to be unintentionally inaccurate, and my experience, opinions and knowledge of living with Parkinson's will inevitably change over time as the disease progresses.

Please remember I am an ordinary person living with an awful disease. I write to put across my personal feelings and experiences and hope that people with Parkinson's feel less alone when dealing with such a misunderstood condition. Also, to try and explain why I am so unpredictable and unreliable as I show the impact it has on every second of every day, twenty-four seven.

In summary please read, watch and listen to all things Parkinality and feel free to think (delete as applicable), "that is interesting/boring/irrelevant/just damn odd/worthless/splendid/amazing/fantastic/funny/weird," but do not act on it (please).

What is Parkinson's Disease (PD)?

Definition from The Cure Parkinson's Trust website:
Parkinson's is a progressive neurological condition – it can be successfully treated with a range of therapies but it is currently incurable. In 2018 around 145,000 people in the UK alone are living with Parkinson's (1 person in every 350). This is expected to increase by 18% by the year 2025 and is set to almost double by 2065. It is estimated that 1 person in 37 will receive a diagnosis of Parkinson's during their lifetime.
The symptoms of Parkinson's are mainly due to the loss of dopamine containing nerve cells in the basal ganglia area of the brain which controls movement. Low levels of dopamine slow the body's movement which make day-to-day activities, such as eating, getting dressed or using everyday objects such as a phone or computer, difficult. The main symptoms of Parkinson's are tremor, muscle stiffness and slowness of movement, but not everyone will experience all of these.
Also, every person's Parkinson's is different, and each person has their own combination of symptoms and side effects, which makes treating Parkinson's difficult – other symptoms such as tiredness, pain and low moods can impact significantly on an individual's day-to-day life. As Parkinson's progresses over time the symptoms generally worsen, impacting on quality of life.

https://www.cureparkinsons.org.uk/aboutparkinsons
Accessed January 2020

What is Young Onset Parkinson's Disease (YOPD)?

Young Onset Parkinson's Disease (YOPD) refers to those diagnosed with Parkinson's Disease (PD) under fifty.
Those diagnosed at a younger age will be living with the disease for longer, giving the symptoms more time to develop/worsen as the brain cells degenerate. They are likely to suffer the side effects from long-term use of the PD medication and will require more advanced treatment.

Medication side effects

Some Parkinson's medications have side effects. If you or a friend or family member notices any changes in habits, moods or symptoms, speak to a medical professional for advice and support. Do not change any medication without consulting a medical professional, and then only under their guidance.

Support

Everyone with Parkinson's is different and everyone needs different types of support. Parkinson's is misunderstood and unpredictable. Living with PD can be very isolating. There is a lot of support out there, please speak to your medical professional for advice.

The Cure Parkinson's Trust

The Cure Parkinson's Trust (CPT) is the only organisation in the UK solely dedicated to finding a cure for Parkinson's. Founded in 2005 by four people living with the condition, CPT takes a patient-centric approach to funding innovative projects and inspirational scientists to modify the progression of Parkinson's and to find a cure. At CPT we believe that we are closer than ever to delivering treatments that for the first time will slow, stop or even reverse the progression of the disease.
https://www.cureparkinsons.org.uk/
Accessed January 2020

Spotlight YOPD

A website for those with YOPD run by those with YOPD
YOPD: Young Onset Parkinson's Disease diagnosed in those under 50
https://www.spotlightyopd.org/
Accessed January 2020

What is Parkinality? (pa:kin-al-i-tee)

Parkinality is a blend word which I created.
Parkin(son's) (person)ality
Parkinson's + Personality = Parkinality

The Parkinality Poet is

A multi-faceted oxymoron with a GSOH.
Her large handbag contains: a blue disabled badge, medication, spare medication, back-up medication, water, disabled bus and train pass, radar key which unlocks ten billion public toilets, an umbrella and two walking sticks. On a Friday night you may find her chatting, dancing and getting up to other general malarkey. We have it on good authority she is not a 'pain in the arse'.
Previous theatre credits include: *Seaweed*, *Tree*, *Lamb* and *The Tin Man* (non-speaking/singing role).

aka Julie Walker

I was diagnosed in 2012, aged forty-four. with Young Onset Parkinson's Disease (YOPD). A (currently) incurable, degenerative neurological condition. I try to remain positive, concentrating on what I can do, rather than dwelling on what I can't.
I am not a doctor or medically trained, merely an ordinary person, dealing with an awful disease.

The aim of this book

I can't cure Parkinson's, but I can raise awareness in the hope that people will gain an insight into this unpredictable, debilitative condition, and ultimately that a cure is found.

Thank you
to every single person who has:

Moved out of my peripheral vision

Laughed with me
Cried with me
Said nothing
Talked

Been there for me
Stood by me
Not rushed me

Let me copy their walk
Offered me their chair
Helped me carry stuff
Picked up my stick

Sung with me
Danced with me
Picked up the phone

Seen the funny side

a special thank you to
E, C, H

and thank you to the Wise Man.

Profound
The Parkinality Poet

I am so much more
than this new facet of me
this thing which they simply
call PD

ISBN: 9781838590895

£8.99

Read about Ralph and his clipboard, Nora with her knitted animals and Tamara and her botox. Some poems are silly, some funny, some sad, some confusing. They will all make you stop and think. Some might educate you and I hope all will entertain.

They simply tell a story and tell a story simply, no technical words or backwards writing to decipher.

I am The Parkinality Poet (aka Janet Bric-a-Brac, aka Julie Walker) and I have written all the poems and performed many to live audiences. All of the 'people' are fictional, they reside in that overcrowded place; 'My Imagination'.

Have a think - have you learnt anything new today?

Lightning Source UK Ltd.
Milton Keynes UK
UKHW020741030320
359644UK00010B/596